The Hour is Coming!

The Theme of Time in the Gospel of John (Part 1)

Dynamic Time:
A force that stimulates change

by Eliza Wright

> 'The only reason for time is so that everything
> doesn't happen at once.'
> Albert Einstein (1879 – 1955)

ISBN: 978-1-78364-565-7

www.obt.org.uk

****

Abbreviations
KJV: The King James Version of the Bible, also known as the Authorised Version or AV. (In this version, words in italics have been added by the translators to improve the sense in English).
LITV: Green's Literal Translation of the Bible.
LXX: The Septuagint, the earliest extant Greek translation of the Old Testament.
NIV: The New International Version of the Bible.
CE: Current era, (previously AD).
BCE: Before current era, (previously BC).

****

The Hour in Coming

Contents

1.
Introduction.

1. Introduction.

In this book, I hope to show the value of themes in the study of Scripture; how the simple starting point of selecting one subject and applying it to a particular text, can be built up into a useful body of knowledge from which we can proceed in many directions. This study focusses on the Theme of Time in the Gospel of John.

Although my first objective is to present my research and the conclusions I have drawn, the second is to encourage readers towards using themes as a basis for investigation. For this reason the study may seem more like a commentary on how the investigation proceeded than as an evidential report followed by results and conclusions. So, I explain what inspired me to begin, and show how I worked through it. I discuss my doubts. The aim is to energise readers towards the idea that they should check up on me and *decide what they think*. It's not rocket science.

To facilitate individual investigation, most of the references I've given are, at the time of writing, easily obtained from the Open Bible Trust, on-line book-stores or the Internet. Also, the general use of themes is covered in an earlier study[1], however an outline of the concept specific to the Theme of Time is given below.

The first confession I should make is that the inquiry turned into a much larger piece of work than I'd envisaged and so has been

---

[1] See my book 'Motive, Method and Opportunity: The Fundamental Elements of Bible Study' in which research methods using characterisation, themes and patterns, are described in detail. The present study is an attempt to demonstrate how those methods work in practice.

divided into two parts. The division attempts to be logical and splits the subject by considering the different ways that the Gospel uses time. Occasionally the two types overlap, but it seemed to me that as I had to draw a line somewhere, this division had some merit.

Part 1: Dynamic Time:

This focusses on things that *change* over the time-scale of the Gospel. They can be thought of as *internal* links to time as they exist within the text. As the story proceeds, situations develop, tensions increase, and people change their minds. Jesus Himself is seen working to regulate the pace of these changes towards 'the hour that is coming', while opposing forces seek to prevent this. Finally, 'the hour has come for the Son of Man to be glorified', and the two sequences converge at the crucifixion.

Part 2: Stationary Time:[2]

These are the things or events whose time-reference *does not change*; that is, they are *external* to the Gospel. So, John could not change the period of time in which he lived and wrote, the time-frame of the ministry of Jesus Christ, or the time or times when his gospel was meant to be read. He could not change differences between the Roman and Jewish way of measuring time, or the words that were then available to him in the Greek language. All these things are the same throughout the Gospel. *We* might have differing opinions about them but that is another matter. Also included in this section is the case where the time-

---

[2] This aspect will be covered by a forthcoming booklet: 'The Theme of Time in the Gospel of John, Part 2'.

scale is so vast as to be incomprehensible to human beings, that is, the frequent references to 'eternal life'.

The scope of this study suggests that time is an important theme in John's Gospel. Time-related ideas are used at every level from mundane statements of the time of day, to important theological concepts such as the idea of 'eternal life' and the momentous and pivotal event of God Himself stepping into time. But before we look at these subjects in more detail, we need to ask...

What is a Theme?

A theme is defined as 'an idea that recurs in or pervades a work of art or literature' (Oxford Dictionaries). Looking at Scripture from the viewpoint of a theme means that we consider a certain text with reference to a particular topic that we have selected.

Themes are useful because they concentrate the mind. They allow us to focus on a specific feature so that we are less likely to lose the thread in a tangle of complications. Also our theme may draw attention to parts of the text we would not otherwise have noticed, or cause us to ask questions we had not thought of before. All this can bring new understanding. It's so easy to glide over a few verses because we know and love them so well that we never stop to consider what the words actually mean, or that there might be an alternative interpretation. This does not mean that familiarity with the whole text is unnecessary, just that we can take it in stages.

Some Features of Themes.

It may be helpful to bear in mind that:

1. A theme may appear in a piece of writing as a deliberate, conscious act of the author, but this is not always the case. All authors have an agenda which may put a certain spin on the message.

2. A theme may not be obvious. It may be cleverly hidden, incorporated on many levels as part of the subtext of the writing.

3. A theme may be an artefact, a coincidence, picked up by the reader entirely as a result of the fact that he or she is looking for it!

4. In Scripture, the theme could have been introduced (subconsciously or otherwise) by inspiration of the Holy Spirit.

5. Looking at one theme is only a beginning. You might find it's bound up with a second, or you might ring the changes by proposing its opposite. Continuing down this path you will open up interesting and connected avenues of research.

6. Themes are not without pitfalls. They can be taken to extremes, when we might fail to see the writing as a whole. So it's important that, before coming to any conclusions, we consider the context of any new ideas we are proposing.

Choosing a Theme.

If you look for themes in John's Gospel via an Internet search engine, you will discover many studies on the ideas that pervade this text, such as love, life, and water to name just a few. At the time I am writing, however, no one seems to have published a study on the Theme of Time itself.

So how did I get the idea? I will call it serendipity, a 'fortunate accident'. My interest was initially sparked by reading 'Jesus and the Eyewitnesses' by Richard Bauckham, in which he mentions that references to 'time' occur at the beginning and ending of John's Gospel.

> John 1:1 NIV **In the beginning** was the Word, and the Word   was with God, and the Word was God.

> John 21:23 NIV   Because of this, the rumour spread among the brothers that this disciple would not die. But Jesus did not say that he would not die; he only said, 'If I want him to remain alive **until I return**, what is that to you?'

I already knew that time figured significantly in John's Gospel because I had recently read an account of the possible discrepancies between this gospel and the other three, which are known as the Synoptic Gospels.[3] So my next move was to read the Gospel again, simply scanning for references to time. This convinced me that an in-depth study of this theme would prove profitable.

The Scope of a Theme.

---

[3] See 'The Four Gospels Compared and Contrasted' by Henry and Penny. A concise attempt to harmonise the accounts can be found in Manley's booklet: 'The Chronology of the Gospel of Jesus Christ'. Other useful books are Humphreys' 'The Mystery of the Lord's Supper' (which concentrates mainly on the last week in the life of the Lord Jesus); Anderson's 'The Riddles of the Fourth Gospel' Chapter 3: 'The Historical Riddles of the Fourth Gospel', and Lincoln's 'The Gospel According to St. John' Introduction pp 26 – 39. Much information is also available on the Internet.

Having settled upon a theme, the next thing is to study that topic as thoroughly as you can. This will probably reveal a much broader scope than you imagined. When I began to investigate 'time', I certainly got more than I bargained for!

It can also help if you consider your topic in a broader setting than that of the Bible. For instance, if I were writing a novel whose theme was time, I might use all manner of time-related details. The ageing of characters, buildings, landscapes; people who let time slip away; people who use every second; the tick of a metronome, the beat of a pulse, the poignancy of a sundial hidden in the gloom of an overgrown garden; once you start thinking about your theme, many ways of interpreting it will present themselves.

After all, time is going to play a background role in every progressive story from 'Three Little Pigs' to 'War and Peace'. So I was looking for something that goes further than the simple re-iteration of 'And then ...'

It's helpful to make a list of all these things, and keep the list open, for I confess that I continue to add to that list even now. The next thing I had to clarify, however, was:

'What then is Time?'

Which is what St Augustine of Hippo asked himself hundreds of years ago. 'If no one asks me,' he decided, 'I know what it is. If I wish to explain it to him who asks, I do not know.'

I have a lot of sympathy with him! Time is an interesting subject, but a scientific discussion about its nature, or details about its measurement, are probably not going to help us much here. So I shall concentrate on the more ordinary aspects of time, things that affect most people all over the world and all down the ages.

At the start of the 21st Century, in the Western world, most of us are acutely aware of time and how it affects our lives. There is a dominant concept of linear time which most of us take for granted. We measure it with ever more sophisticated clocks and grudgingly accept its rule over our lives. We plan our use of it on calendars and timetables, but are always running out of it. Our lives are lived 'against the clock'.

Others have time on their hands that they do not know what to do with. This may be due to illness, or the anticipation of an event of such magnitude that life is put on hold until it occurs.

Also there are the changes that the passing of time brings. The machines we rely upon, and parts of ourselves as well, begin to wear out and no longer function properly.

So because it passes too quickly or too slowly, and it frequently brings unwelcome changes that often cannot be undone, we tend to view time as an enemy.

It seems to me that most people in 1st Century Palestine would have thought the same, despite their lack of digital timepieces and automatic alarms. This is an interesting concept, as it forms a link between ourselves and the people who inhabit John's Gospel. Some are busy-busy, some are deliberating in the shade of a fig tree. Some are in the wrong place at the wrong time, some feel that time is running out. Others may wonder how much longer they can keep going, or speculate on the trials that the coming 'night' is going to bring, or decide to cool the situation by taking some time out.

So, as I began my study, I was thinking of time in the familiar way; the progression of minutes, hours, days, weeks, and months that hour-glasses, sundials, pendulums, calendars and generations have measured for thousands of years. This is also the way that the passage of time is recorded in the Gospel.

Measuring Time.

Measuring time is for us very easy. In 1st century Palestine it would have been rather different in that the general population would not have had one eye on their digital time-piece, but on light-levels and shadows. However, with practice it is surprising how accurate you can be using these clues.

The earliest information we have about measuring time involves shadow clocks and sundials. A shadow clock has been found which was used in Egypt in the second millennium BCE. Sundials evolved from this and one is mentioned in the Old Testament book of Isaiah 38:8.

In the first century CE, the Romans continued to use sundials and also water-clocks, which had the advantage of not depending on light or the visibility of stars and so could be used at night. (Sand-timers and mechanical clocks were not invented until much later).[4]

The Jews of that period seem to have used observation rather than gadgets. The arrival of 'dawn', the position of the sun, and the appearance of certain stars after sunset defined their day.

---

[4] See Richards: 'Mapping Time – the Calendar and its History', and Cupcea: 'Timekeeping in the Roman Army'.

Significant Words.

Significant or 'key' words that relate to the theme are very important. In my original research, I looked at how these words were used in the KJV and the NIV, but it's also important to consider the language in which the text was originally written, and the opinions of a range of scholars. This matter because translators don't always agree, and this may obscure a valuable reference.[5] Here is a brief resumé of some of the words that pertain to time in the original Greek:

1. Age and Eternity:

>   (1) *aion* (Strong: G165) an age, perpetuity, eternity.

>   (2) *aionios* (Strong: G166) eternal, forever, everlasting.

2. An Hour: *horah* (Strong: G5610) an hour, day, instant. It is usually translated 'hour' in the KJV, but sometimes as time or as an estimate of the time of day in more modern translations.

3. A Set Time: *kairos* (Strong: G2540) an occasion, a set or proper time, a season.

4. An Indefinite Period of Time: *kronos* (Strong: G5550) a season, a space of time, a period, an opportunity. Mostly this is used in a non-specific way, such as: 'a little while', 'a long time' etc.

In the case of the Theme of Time, we can divide the investigation broadly into two groups: *Firstly*, words that describe what time it actually is, was or will be, such as: 'day', 'morning', 'the tenth

---

[5] I use Strong's Concordance and Vine's Expository Dictionary as a starting point. They both cover the Old and New Testaments, and both are available on line.

hour', 'next week', 'the Sabbath', 'the last day'. *Secondly*, words that more express ideas related to time, such as 'eternity', 'forever', a 'season', the 'fateful hour', an 'occasion'.

Time in John's Gospel – an Overview

So, we now have a subject for the theme: 'time', and a text to apply it to: 'John's Gospel'.[6] Clearly, before we proceed, some acquaintance with this part of Scripture is recommended. I would suggest an initial read-through, looking out for any words that seem to refer to time.

Some of the ways John uses time are straightforward and are easy to spot. For example, he tells us the day and the hour, so we have a sense of time passing, e.g. in John 2:1 he tells us that on the third day, a wedding took place at Cana in Galilee.

Words such as morning, evening, night, early, late, now, dark etc. can be used in this way, also terms such as 'the Sabbath' or the name of a feast such as Passover or Pentecost.

As I have already pointed out above, time marks and pins down the beginning and end of the Gospel (John 1:1 and John 21:23).

Looking more closely we find that time markers are used to add credibility and depth to the text. To make you feel you are there, e.g. in John 10:22 we are told that it was the Feast of Dedication and it was winter. Later, after the crucifixion, in John 20:1 we

---

[6] I should point out here that the differences between John's Gospel and the Synoptic Gospels, although they involve time in the sense of a different chronology of events, do not form part of this study except for one aspect, which will be discussed in Chapter 5.

have Mary Magdalene walking in the early morning, on the first day of the week, while it was still dark.

Going deeper still, we can see the emotional effects of time in the reactions of the people portrayed. 'Please come to my son now, or he will die!' begs the royal official (John 4:47).'If only you'd got here sooner!' cry Mary and Martha, (John 11:21, 32). Many of John's signs have a time-dependant aspect, as we shall see in the next chapter.

In preparation for this I suggest reading through the miraculous signs in John's Gospel again, and for each one consider how people might have reacted to what happened, in particular looking for aspects or feelings that relate to time.

As to which of the many gospel events are signs, scholars have come to different conclusions, but by and large they agree that some or all of the following events, constitute 'signs':

1) The marriage in Cana, where water becomes wine (2:1 – 11).
2) The healing of the official's acutely sick son (4:46 – 54).
3) The healing of the chronically sick man at the Pool of Bethesda (5:1 – 15).
4) The feeding of 5000 families on 5 loaves and 2 fishes (6:1 – 15).
5) The Lord Jesus walks on water (6:16 – 21).
6) The healing of the man born blind at the Pool of Siloam (9:1 – 38).
7) The resurrection of Lazarus (11:1 – 46).
8) The Resurrection of the Lord (20:1 – 18).
9) The Draught of 153 Fishes (21:1 – 11).

Before you begin, remember that blending a theme into a piece of writing means incorporating it at every level, and so it is at every level that you must look in order to extract it. Do not be afraid to use your imagination.

'Why me? Why now?' the man who'd been sick 38 years might have thought. 'Why couldn't this have happened when I was younger and would have had the time and energy to make something of myself?' (John 5:1 – 15).

Of course, I hope it goes without saying that, having used your imagination, you must then scrutinise the text to ensure that nothing you have ascribed to the event in question contravenes Scripture!

2.
Waiting.

2. Waiting.

Readers may be forgiven for wondering why, at the start of a study on time as a dynamic force, I have chosen to begin with a chapter on waiting. What on earth is dynamic about waiting? It brings to mind huddling in draughty bus-shelters or turning the pages of dog-eared magazines as we anticipate the attention of the doctor.

But waiting has always seemed to me to be a fundamental aspect of Christianity, and at the same time it is one of the most difficult roles we have to undertake as Christians. It is a state of being which the human race (myself included!) seems particularly ill-equipped to deal with, perhaps because it's so easy to assume the attitude described above.

In fact, waiting can take many forms and we see them illustrated in John's Gospel in various ways. The Signs in particular highlight waiting at a personal level, to which most of us can easily relate. We can surely empathise with the plight of the sick man and the blind man, waiting many years for their personal miracle, probably having given up hope of ever finding a cure. We can feel the urgency of the nobleman whose son was critically ill, of the disciples tossed by the storm, of Mary and Martha thinking in despair: 'If only the Lord were here!'

Then there is the waiting experienced by all of the Lord's disciples and followers after the crucifixion, a kind of bewildered, hopeless waiting, since it is apparent that none of them actually expected the Lord to arise from the dead. Most of us will have had similar experiences. Minutes stretch into hours, and days into

weeks, as we wait for that awful or wonderful event to materialise
... or not.

In the first few centuries of the Christian era, some believers fled
into the deserts of Egypt to wait and pray for the Lord's second
coming. To pass the time they adopted a rhythmic though rather
pointless activity of weaving mats one day, and un-weaving them
the next. Apart from giving them 'something to do with their
hands', it is hard to see how they imagined it would help.
Eventually, some weavers realised that Jesus would come when
His time was right, so they kept their mats, sold them in the
market place, and witnessed their faith as they did so. I am sure
that this would have made their waiting much easier. It's
encouraging to know you're doing something useful, both for
God and for other people.[7]

And that is part of the problem. Of course, we are all waiting, one
way or another, for the Lord's second coming, but for most of us
this is not the wait that causes us frustration and impatience.
These feelings are likely caused more by our inextinguishable
need to 'do something useful' and for that something to have a
positive result. While this is commendable, it is partly our
aversion to waiting that enables the Enemy to use time to foil
God's plans, and our innate impatience means that we all too
easily fall into the trap.

Our very human failure, to want it all *now*, is by no means a
modern phenomenon. It has often been the cause of problems in
the working out of God's plan, e.g.:

1) Adam and Eve could not wait to attain 'knowledge' in the
Lord's good time (Genesis 3:6).

---

[7] William Griffin, 'Endtime'. See Celtic Daily Prayer p 723.

2) Abraham and Sarah could not wait for the Lord to fulfil their wish for a son (Genesis 16:2).

3) The Israelites could not wait for Moses to come down from the mountain (Exodus 32:1).

4) Impatience may have been one of the motives behind Judas' betrayal.

Of course, we do not all have an obvious opportunity to witness and this can be very frustrating. Most people will have heard John Milton's famous line: 'They also serve who only stand and wait.' Here, Milton is speaking about himself. Blindness had taken away his ability to witness the best way he thought he could, and he was waiting for God to reveal to him how else he might serve.

The Meaning of the word 'Wait'.

Linked to the above is the fact that the verb 'to wait' in English can mean two things:

1) To stay in one place and remain inactive in expectation of something, to hold oneself in a state of perpetual readiness. This is where boredom, frustration and thumb-twiddling thrive.

2) To act as a waiter, that is to be ready to serve when the time comes. This kind of waiting is linked to the word 'minister'. To be ready is the clue: good waiters in restaurants don't just stand there, they look for signals from both customer and kitchen, and prepare in advance items that might be needed. They wait actively, not

passively. To know that we have to wait does not mean we must do so in idleness or in pointless activity.

Waiting and Watching.

These two ideas go together almost without saying. Anyone who waits is waiting for something to happen. To make sure they don't miss it, they have to keep alert. They have to watch.

> Micah 7:7 NIV But as for me, I watch in hope for the LORD, I wait for God my Saviour; my God will hear me.

> Matthew 25:13 NIV 'Therefore keep watch, because you do not know the day or the hour.'

> Mark 13:33 NIV Be on guard! Be alert! You do not know when that time will come.

As a psychiatric nurse on night duty, I spent many solitary hours watching and waiting, but I soon discovered that if that's all you do, you end up nodding off! Deciphering case notes and reading text books, however, keeps you awake, prepared and incidentally more able to pass your exams! This is just the kind of watching and waiting we have as Christians, though I should probably add that careful preparation does not guarantee that the anticipated event won't come out of the blue and take you by surprise!

It will surely come as no surprise, however, that John's Gospel takes a slightly different line. In John 3:29, John the Baptist is not watching and waiting for the bridegroom, but *listening and waiting,* waiting for the bridegroom's *words.*

Waiting in John's Gospel.

People wait in all sorts of ways in John's Gospel, but trying to pick out connections with exact words is difficult. The English word 'wait' and its derivatives occur four times in the NIV translation, only two of which could pertain to the kind of waiting we're interested in, the sort where the subject is waiting for something important but its arrival could be any time or possibly never. One was mentioned above (John 3:29) and the other is John 5:3, where disabled people wait by the Pool of Siloam. But the Greek word so translated occurs 21 times, and there are several others that have similar meanings which also may be translated in more than one way into English.

So rather than do the usual word study, instead I looked for situations where the kind of waiting I was interested in was implied. I found that almost all the Signs are linked by implication to waiting, so is there anything we can learn from them about this 'activity'?

Going back to the chronically sick man of John 5:1 – 15, mentioned at the end of Chapter 1, I suggested you use your imagination to explore his character and experience how he felt. Now some Christians won't approve of this tactic, and I agree that it's speculative and we can't prove any of it, but on the other hand it can bring new life to a text that has become moribund in the retelling. Also it can spark enthusiasm for learning about life and culture in New Testament times, or give you an insight that you hadn't thought of before. So let's try it and see where it takes us:

1) The man has been ill for 38 years, so must be at least that old, possibly much older. He's therefore quite an old man for that time. He can't move about with ease, and years of

inactivity could have caused his muscles to atrophy and a number of other physiological problems. He's probably in quite a bad way.

2) Yet he's still alive, and still people are willing to convey him to the Pool of Bethesda. Having no one to help him into the water, he probably goes there to beg. This also implies that he has no family.

3) The Lord gives him a choice. 'Do you want to get well?' This is not a silly question. Getting well would mean that he would not be able to beg. What's he going to do for a living, at his age?

4) Yet the man goes for it... and walks off with his mat into a culture shock that must have been immense.

But from this account we learn the value of dogged persistence while we wait, (compare the parable of the workers in the vineyard, some of whom have to wait all day to be hired, Matthew 20:1 – 16). Also it implies that the man's waiting was not undertaken in idleness or he would surely have died of depression if not from hypostatic complications like pneumonia. He keeps himself going, hoping for a better future, and when the chance comes shows considerable bravery in electing to be healed. True, he doesn't stand up to the Jews like the blind man does later (9:1 – 38), but this might simply be the result of a life of illness, solitude and loss of confidence. Did he put his faith in Jesus? Did he survive? Did he starve? As with many of the gospel stories, we're not told what happened in the end.

Going through the gospel in detail provides the following clues as to how we might wait and how we might react when the time comes for action.

1) Wait patiently, tenaciously and actively for the right moment to arrive.

2) Recognise that timing may be critical, and the Lord's timing is often different to ours (see Chapters 4 and 5 below). More may be at stake than we realise. Death is not the end, and with God anything is possible.

3) Bravery may be required when that moment comes, as well as a willingness to adapt to new situations.

Which is all very well, but the next question is one that must have puzzled most of us at some time or other: What exactly is God telling us to do? Is He saying 'Go!' or are we being impatient? Is He saying 'Stay!' or have we become lazy and too stuck in our rut?

A Question of Balance.

There has to be a balance between the possible inertia of waiting and the call to action. In my opinion our preparations are the key; they keep us active as well as prepared. You can never have too much learning on and around the subject of Christianity.

When Paul was in prison, even during his last imprisonment in Rome, he did not waste his time but carried on studying, learning and writing as best he could. 'When you come bring... the books' he tells Timothy (2 Tim 4:13 KJV). Charles Spurgeon makes the following (abridged) comments:

'He's inspired, and yet he wants books! He's been preaching for thirty years, and yet he wants books! He's seen the Lord, and yet he wants books! ... He's written the major part of the New Testament, and yet he wants books!'[8]

If we have no obvious opportunity to serve God now and are waiting in the hope that He will one day find us employment, then clearly something must occur between those two states. Something must change. This could be a change in our circumstances or that of the world in which we live. Or, it might be a change in our perception, so that what seemed to be an impenetrable brick wall is revealed to have a hidden doorway. Or the change may be that we now know enough to move on. Whatever the change is, it will give us a new perspective so that we know we are on the way.

Waiting also, perhaps, requires us to be available to act when the call comes.

And it's possible there is an element of instinct in all this. Mary Magdalene was presumably acting out of instinct when she waited behind at the tomb. She couldn't believe that was it. And she was right. Peter also was acting on instinct when he denied that he knew Jesus: his instinct for survival was at work! Later, he was to feel bitterly sorry for his actions, but consider what a tremendous part Peter has played in the survival of the Christian church, all because *he* survived to fight another day! And not least, his predicament and how he responded to it has encouraged those of us who have sometimes made the wrong call.

---

[8] For the whole thing see Spurgeon (1834 – 1892): 'Spurgeon's Expository Encyclopaedia' 11:386.

Redeeming the Time.

Readers familiar with the King James Version of the Bible may have come across the phrase 'redeeming the time'. It does not occur in John's Gospel, but in two of Paul's letters (Ephesians 5:16 and Colossians 4:5). It is an exhortation by Paul as to how Christians should live. I bring it up here because I think it's an effective description of how we should try to use our time and our skills both while we are waiting and afterwards. In the NIV translation the phrase 'redeeming the time' is translated 'making the most of every opportunity'.

> Ephesians 5:15-16 KJV See then that ye walk circumspectly, not as fools, but as wise, redeeming the time, because the days are evil.

> Ephesians 5:15-16 NIV Be very careful, then, how you live—not as unwise but as wise, making the most of every opportunity, because the days are evil.

Pause for a moment to think about why the KJV translation uses 'redeem' and the NIV 'make the most of'. Often the KJV is just using rather old-fashioned English, but sometimes, and this is one of them, we lose in the more modern translation the subtlety of what that old-fashioned word implies. So, as is often the case, it helps to go back to the Greek. Here we find the Greek word *exagorazo* (G1805) is used. It literally means 'out of the market place'. The idea is that you buy something from the market, and thus *take it off the market.* No one else can buy it. It's used in only two other places in the New Testament, Galatians 3:13 ('Christ redeemed us from the curse of the Law') and Galatians 4:5 ('so that He might redeem those who were under the Law'). The term was used for buying slaves. So we might say that Christ purchased us out of our slavery. He paid the price in order to take us out of a grim situation, to take us out of the market place where we might be 'bought' by someone with less benevolent motives.

But here *we* are told that we should be redeeming *time* (or taking an opportunity). What sort of time? What kind of opportunity? We've looked at the word *kairos* earlier, and it's that word which is used here. So we can say,

1) It refers to an occasion, a proper or right time, a point in time, a season. The length is not specified, it could be lunch time or harvest time. The significant factor is, if you turn up at the refectory at 3.30 p.m. you've missed your lunch; if you're on holiday at harvest time you've lost your crop. It's vanished time *that you can never make up.*

2) Therefore what we are being asked to do is redeem a time or take an opportunity that, if we don't act promptly, *will be lost.* And what is worse, someone else might use it for nefarious purposes.

3) Why? Because the days are evil. (All the translations agree about that!) This is as true now as it was in Paul's day. We must beware of our opportunities sliding away into the darkness, and not only due to the many worldly problems we might have to contend with. Our time on Earth is limited; our time-opportunities to make a difference are more limited still. Any way the Enemy can contrive to reduce it further, and to give us impossible choices as to how we use our time, he will do it, you can bet.

As John's Gospel puts it, 'Night is coming, when no one can work' (John 9:4). For us it has been 'night' for nearly 2000 years.

Yet the Lord continues, 'While I am in the world, I am the Light of the World' (John 9:5). And Paul tells us that Christ may dwell in our hearts through faith (Ephesians 3:17). So, through our faith, Christ is still here, living within us. He is still illuminating the world. Because the Light is still here, however dim it may be compared to His own direct Light, redeeming the time is still possible.

3.
Time,
Cause and
Effect.

3. Time, Cause and Effect.

Some scholars seem to think that John's Gospel was not written in chronological sequence; that is, events did not occur in real time in the order in which they appear in the gospel. Certainly, the chronology is different to that of the Synoptics and many attempts have been made to iron out the apparent discrepancies, as has been noted above. A common theory is that the events John describes were selected by him to illustrate certain theological points, and so they do not necessarily follow the actual sequence in which they occurred.

Whether or not this is so, I believe it is possible to show that John did not always disregard the natural time line. To illustrate this, I have followed the interactions between Jesus and a group John calls 'the Jews'. Observing the changes in the way people act, and how they behave towards each other, shows that these changes are logical and progressive. This supports the idea that the scenes are chronological.

Who are 'the Jews' of John's Gospel?

The term 'the Jews' (Greek: *hoi Iudaioi*) is another aspect of this Gospel that could be studied as a theme. If we include the three references to the term in the singular, it is found 72 times, as compared with five times in Matthew and Luke, and six in Mark. Space does not permit such an in-depth survey, but our first task must be to ask: to whom is John referring when he speaks, sometimes in a very disparaging way, of 'the Jews'? Unfortunately, John does not categorically define them. In the same way that he does not always tell us which events are signs, he makes us examine the text and discover the clues for ourselves.

The obvious assumption is that it is simply a sweeping generality, and that he means any and all Jews as distinct from any other ethnic grouping. This seems to have been the way that the term *hoi Iudaioi* would have been used at the time.[9] But a careful reading of the Gospel shows that there has to be more to it than that. For a start, Jesus Himself is a Jew and is recognised as such (4:9). He attends Jewish feasts (5:1; 7:10; 12:12). He is buried in accordance with Jewish customs (19:40). Yet clearly He has little in common with the group of Jews who constantly oppose Him. At one point He describes them as belonging to 'your father, the devil' (8:44), an accusation which is difficult to square with the statement given to the Samaritan woman, that 'salvation is from the Jews' (4:22)!

So we have to conclude that when John uses the term 'the Jews' he is not always referring to exactly the same group of people. The phrase can have a variety of meanings, and the differences depend on the context. It seems to be one of the several ways John has devised to get his readers or hearers to use their brains!

In my view we can divide John's use of 'the Jews' into two main groups. The first covers largely descriptive uses pertaining to the Jewish national identity and religion e.g.

> John 2:6 NIV Nearby stood six stone water jars, the kind used by the Jews for ceremonial washing, each holding from twenty to thirty gallons.

> John 6:4 KJV And the passover, a feast of the Jews, was

---

[9] See Lincoln pp 70 – 81.

nigh.

The second use has the term refer to a specific group of people, characters who are part of the action of the Gospel. Put that way, you might be forgiven for expecting this group to have uniformity in their outlook and reactions, but the text does not confirm this. What we find is that they are a group of people who, though they follow more or less the Jewish religion, encompass a whole range of personalities and levels of belief, particularly with regard to their feelings about Jesus. Their opposition varies from asking valid questions, to heated arguments and threats; from reasonable doubt to physical violence and finally murder.

When John talks about 'the Jews', it's as if he's deliberately pointing out their diversity, and equally importantly, he shows how group dynamics work. People fear those who seem to them to be the more immediate threat. If our Lord had wanted an enormous following of sycophants He could have walked the earth invincibly striking dead all those who did not believe in Him. But that (thankfully) is not His way. Unfortunately, this leaves *us* with a power-gap, and it seems there is no shortage of individuals willing to set aside whatever principles they have in order to dive into it.

In the case of John's Gospel the people with power (apart from the Romans), are firstly the Jewish religious leaders, but secondly, the 'crowd', the ordinary people. Either or both of these together can be referred to by John as 'the Jews'. Either can have members who are for Jesus or against Him.

> John 10:19-21 NIV At these words the Jews (*Pharisees, 9:40*) were again divided. Many of them said, 'He is demon-possessed and raving mad. Why listen to him?' But

others said, 'These are not the sayings of a man possessed by a demon. Can a demon open the eyes of the blind?'

And either can take actions that can have unpleasant consequences:

> John 11:45-46 NIV Therefore many of the Jews (*ordinary Jews*, not *the Pharisees*) who had come to visit Mary, and had seen what Jesus did, put their faith in him. But some of them went to the Pharisees and told them what Jesus had done.

Over the whole Gospel, only about half the references to 'the Jews' show them as hostile to Jesus. But as we shall see, as the Gospel progresses, the balance shifts towards increasing antagonism and greater involvement of the Jewish authorities, upon whom John finally focusses.[10] This subgroup show the following features:

1) They are very concerned about keeping the Law and doing everything according to the Law (1:19 – 28; 5:10; 9:16; 18:28).

2) They do not consider there is any possibility that Jesus *was* sent by God, that He actually could be their Messiah; they seem more concerned about their position in society and the privileges this affords them (7:27; 7:47 – 52; 9:22; 11:48).

---

[10] Further information about who 'the Jews' might have been, and John's attitude to them, can be found in the section on 'John and the Jews' in 'The Gospel of John and Christian Theology'. The first two papers give views from two different perspectives.

3) They ask for 'signs' but evidently do not consider the miracles that Jesus did were sufficient (2:18; 12:37).

4) They are so confident they are right they won't listen to anyone else (7:46 – 52; 9:30 – 34).

5) Both ordinary Jews and also other members of the Jewish hierarchy are afraid of them (9:22; 12:42).
6) They have the ear of the High Priest (11:47 – 53).

It is this subgroup of Jews that I would like to follow in this study. If you select the scenes where questioning and antagonism from 'the Jews' occurs, and lay them out in the order in which they appear in the Gospel, you can see a linear pattern emerge. Sometimes this is cause and effect, sometimes it is the gradual change in the way people view each other as time progresses and events unfold which become steadily more significant. What follows is a list of the main scenes of interaction, (in the order they occur in the Gospel), between Jesus, His associates, and 'the Jews'.

1. Seeds of Conflict

There is no overt conflict in Chapter 1, but John leaves us in no doubt there is going to be trouble. Its seeds are planted right from the start (John 1:10,11). We soon learn that John the Baptist has become the focus of attention of 'certain Jews' who send priests, Levites and Pharisees to investigate. Who are you, they ask? On what authority are you baptising and telling people to repent? (1:19 – 25). John's mission statement is comprehensive, but it's not clear when Jesus' baptism actually took place or if the Pharisees who questioned John were there the whole time, since the declaration seems to be spread over three days (1:26 – 36). In summary, John states that:

'I am not the Messiah, or Elijah, or any other prophet. I am here, baptising with water, in order to recognise a certain man and reveal His identity to the nation of Israel. This man is much more important than I am. He will baptise with the Holy Spirit and take away the sin of the world.'

We are not told their reaction to his reply, but I would guess at this stage they decide interest in him will soon fade. 'We'll keep an eye on him,' they probably thought. 'And as for the one he says is coming after him, who is greater, and who baptises with the Holy Spirit, well! Whoever heard of such a thing?'

When John the Baptist proclaims that Jesus of Nazareth is the Lamb of God who takes away the sin of the world (1:29), and who is also the Son of God (1:34), 'the Jews' start watching this newcomer too. But so far 'the Jews' just seem to be checking up on people who think they can go around performing religious rituals without the proper authority. It's a reasonable thing for them to do. It shows us they're taking notice, but it's not a hostile act.

2. Nicodemus, a ruler of 'the Jews'

The next controversy occurs in the temple at Jerusalem (John 2:13 – 22) and is probably quite a shock to the people selling animals, and the money changers, not to mention 'the Jews'. They question Jesus again about His authority, they ask for a 'sign', but they don't understand His answer and they don't take any action. Considering Jesus has just caused chaos in the temple courts they seem quite laid back about the whole thing.

However, following on from this, a Pharisee and ruler comes at night to ask more questions (3:1 – 21). It isn't clear whose side Nicodemus is on at this point. Has he come of his own volition or was he sent by the Temple authorities? Either way, Nicodemus presumably takes away some spark of light from the interview. Later on (7:51) he tentatively takes Jesus' side against the other Pharisees, and by the end of the gospel he is ready to put his life at risk to give this 'teacher come from God' a decent burial (19:39). This is a skilful and possibly brave manoeuvre on the part of John, to allow the introduction of such a character, and in such a way that the reader is ambivalent about him. At this point we cannot tell whether Nicodemus is a potential friend or a spy, but we have the hint that perhaps not all 'the Jews' feel the same way.[11]

3. 'He must become greater; I must become less'

Jesus' disciples begin to baptise, and the Pharisees are informed that He's attracting even more people than John the Baptist (3:22 – 36). They try to use this information to drive a wedge between John the Baptist and Jesus, but they fail. We're not told what else they did, just that the Lord knew they were out to make trouble, and because of this He moved on.

---

[11] Please be assured I am not implying that John made up his characters and that this event did not really happen! However, John had obviously witnessed many incidents and been told about many more. He could not put them all in the gospel and therefore had to be selective. Why would he select a dithering Pharisee, who eventually makes up his mind to believe the Lord, if he was out to imply that all 'the Jews' were out to get Him?

4. 'Pick up your mat and walk'

Here we have the first real sign of antagonism from 'the Jews'. It begins after the healing of the chronically sick man by the Pool of Bethesda (5:1 – 47). Clearly they are more interested in the fact that the rules have been broken (because it is the Sabbath) than that a miracle has been performed and a sick man is now well. Their reaction shows anger and potential violence. Jesus' explanation incenses them even more, for it reveals that He considers Himself equal with God. In fairness to 'the Jews', these two items would have seemed totally sacrilegious to them. The problem is more the fact that they are so steeped in the Law, and obedience to it, that they never stop to think about what Jesus is telling them. 'Had you believed Moses you would have believed me,' Jesus says, 'for he wrote of me.' But they are not listening. As people flock to the Lord Jesus and He performs marvellous signs, 'the Jews' gradually become more hostile, and also, gradually, more afraid. Not only do they fear the challenge to their position, but their precarious stability under Roman rule could be undermined as well.

5. Bread from Heaven?

After the Feeding of the 5000, the Lord goes to the synagogue in Capernaum (6:24 – 71), where 'the Jews' then attack His roots: 'This is Jesus, Joseph's son! How come he's telling us he comes from heaven? What does he mean, he's the bread of heaven and we have to eat his flesh and drink his blood?! The man's mad!' And again, to be fair to 'the Jews', quite a number of Jesus' disciples couldn't stomach it either. Drinking any creature's blood would certainly be anathema to any Jew (Lev 17:14). Clearly allegory was not what these Jews, at any rate, were used to.[12]

6. No Prophet comes out of Galilee!

At the Feast of Tabernacles there's a subtle shift in behaviour of 'the Jews' (7:11 – 53). This time they're looking out for Him. Yet, as He teaches in the Temple, some of them are forced to admire His knowledge of Scripture. The ordinary people are beginning to discuss His ideas too, which alarms the chief priests and Pharisees so much that they send their officers to arrest Him. But even the officers are astounded. 'We've never heard anyone speak like He does!' they report, returning empty-handed. We also see that Nicodemus is among these Jews, and challenges what they are doing.

7. Whoever is without sin, let him throw the first stone!

Now 'the Jews' try another tack (8:1 – 11). Force hasn't worked, and clearly many of the people have come to realise that Jesus, at the very least, is a special person. There would probably be a riot if they tried to arrest Him now. How a group of religious leaders actually managed to 'catch' a woman in the act of adultery, why they caught the woman and not the man, and a few other interesting questions, are beyond the scope of our study. However, it is worth pointing out that the tension has gone up several notches. Not only do 'the Jews' in the form of teachers and Pharisees want to catch Jesus out, they are willing to risk

---

[12] However, Proverbs 9:1 – 6 shows that the idea of eating and drinking being synonymous with taking in knowledge and wisdom was not entirely unknown to them.

having someone who is possibly innocent murdered in a horrible way in order to do it.

8. 'If you knew me, you would know my Father also.'

Outsmarted again, 'the Jews' this time try a legal offensive, (8:13 – 20). 'Here you are, appearing as your own witness! Your testimony is not valid.' A battle of wits follows. Jesus is accused of being not only mad but a Samaritan. 'The Jews' are accused of being just like their father, the devil, the father of lies. In the end 'the Jews' pick up stones, prepared to carry out what has up to now been a threat. If Jesus had not managed to disappear among the crowds, those stones might have found their mark.

9. 'I was blind but now I see!'

A while later, by the Pool of Siloam, Jesus heals a man who was born blind (9:1 – 41). This set piece has two interesting features beside the reaction of 'the Jews'. It is the scene of two changes:

> (1) Jesus indicates that time is running out.
> (2) The recipient of the healing goes out of his way to challenge 'the Jews'. So much so that he is thrown out of the Temple. Apart from Jesus, he is the third person up to now to challenge them, (John the Baptist (3:25 – 36) and Nicodemus (7:51) are the other two, and Pilate challenges them repeatedly later on).

As for 'the Jews', they have been humiliated twice:

(1) By the argument of a 'nobody'. It's clear that the blind man's parents are fearful of 'the Jews', and equally clear that he, although he has up to now been physically blind, has an independent mind and is not afraid.

(2) By Jesus, who tells them: 'If you were blind, you would not be guilty of sin; but now that you claim you can see, your guilt remains.'

10. 'Now a man named Lazarus was sick...'

The Jews' threats rumble on through Chapter 10, but in Chapter 11 the pace suddenly escalates with the raising of Lazarus (11:1 – 53). The Lord ups the ante by ensuring no one can declare this miracle to be a trick. He arrives 'too late'. Lazarus has been dead four days and he smells awful.[13]

Plenty of Jews are in attendance, some no doubt honestly there to support Mary and Martha, others perhaps waiting to see what happens when Jesus arrives, as He surely will, for members of this family are known to be His friends. This group of Jews seems to be ordinary people, not members of the religious hierarchy; many of them are convinced by this impressive miracle that Jesus is the Messiah, but others, perhaps, find it disturbing.

Either way, this is not a story you can bury. Some of the witnessing Jews report to the Pharisees. This would have been a reasonable thing to do. A man possessing powers like this is

---

[13] See the forthcoming booklet 'The Theme of Time in the Gospel of John, Part 2', for a more detailed account of why this was important.

obviously going to create great excitement among the people. On the other hand, if it is a trick, then the sooner this person and his associates are dealt with the better.

So the Pharisees are told and they and the Chief Priests call a meeting of the Sanhedrin. It is of interest that not even this group of Jews seems to be in any doubt that Jesus is performing miracles. 'If we let him go on like this,' they declare, 'everyone will believe in him, and the resulting instability will persuade the Romans to take away both our place and our nation!' Actually, their fear was quite reasonable from a political perspective, and thus the threat rises to the highest level. The High Priest Caiaphas states his opinion and he determines that there will be no debate about the situation. 'You know nothing!' he tells them. 'The case is clear. Our Nation and way of life are both at risk from this man. He must be silenced. It is better that he should die than that our people and culture should be jeopardised.' Caiaphas clearly has no concept of the irony of his statement that Jesus should die for the sake of the nation.

> John 11:53 NIV So from that day on they plotted to take his life.

11. Malice Aforethought! (Numbers 35:20-21)

After the raising of Lazarus, most of John's references to 'the Jews' as active participants in the story now mostly indicate those in the religious hierarchy who, for whatever reason, are seriously scheming to get rid of Jesus. And not only Him; they also have their eye now on Lazarus, the living proof of the stupendous power of His miracles.

It's six days before Passover, and many people are at Jerusalem for the feast. A large number have been convinced by the testimony of those who saw what happened at Bethany. The Pharisees are furious and possibly a bit frightened of the mob. 'Look how the whole world has gone after him!' they exclaim. But now two things happen that tip the balance back towards 'the Jews' and heighten the suspense:

> (1) Many of the Jewish leaders are beginning to believe that the man from Galilee is indeed someone out of the ordinary, but they keep quiet because of their fear of the Pharisees and of losing their position. An example of good men doing nothing (12:42 – 43).

> (2) One of the Lord's own disciples proves to be a turncoat (13:2). 'I can lead you to a sanctuary in the olive groves where Jesus goes to get away from the crowds,' Judas promises 'the Jews'. 'There, you can arrest Him without making a big fuss.'

Thus Jesus is arrested and interrogated by Annas and his son-in-law, Caiaphas the High Priest (18:12 – 27). We already know (11:49 – 50) that Caiaphas considers Jesus' death to be the most convenient way forward for all of them.

This scene is interspersed with flashes back to the courtyard, where Peter is repeatedly denying that he ever knew the prisoner. In a way the whole section is steeped in denial; denial of justice. We know that guilt or innocence will not come into the verdict; it's a foregone conclusion. Meanwhile 'the Jews', not content with any punishment that falls short of execution, now see a way to get the best of both worlds. Their victim will die, and if anyone is ever held to account for this – most unlikely but you never know – it will be the Romans!

12. 'What is Truth?'

So 'the Jews' hand the Lord Jesus over to the Roman Governor, Pontius Pilate (18:28). Normally Pilate would be miles away in Caesarea Maritima but because of the surge of worshippers visiting for the Passover, he's here in Jerusalem in case things get out of hand.[14] 'The Jews' must at first have considered Pilate's presence to be a bonus. Pilate, however, turns out not to be the pushover they had hoped for and he challenges them. It is only when they start hinting that no friend of Caesar would contemplate Jesus' release that Pilate gives in (19:12). The depths to which 'the Jews' have now sunk is underlined by this statement. One of the reasons they would not accept Jesus as their Messiah was that they wanted a military leader who would vanquish the Romans and restore their independence.

Pilate is not stupid and probably realises he's been outmanoeuvred. His uneasy acquiescence is emphasised by his multiple attempts to get Jesus freed and ultimately the writing of the sign in three languages (19:19). Later, he grants permission so that Joseph of Arimathea and Nicodemus can take away the body for burial (19:38). All through Chapter 19 we can feel Pilate's ferment of indecision, his internal conflict.

13. Aftermath.

John does not tell us directly what 'the Jews' did after they had achieved their aim. They would certainly be apprehensive after learning that the body had disappeared, and it's obvious that the remaining disciples continued to fear them (20:19). Matthew tells us that the chief priests and elders plotted with the soldiers

---

[14] See: 'The Archaeology of the Bible', p 155.

guarding the tomb and bribed them to lie about what happened (Matthew 28:11 – 15). Oddly, the lie makes no sense. If the guards had really slept through it all, they could not know how the body left the tomb. We are also told how 'the Jews' dealt with Judas afterwards, and their attitude to the plight of this person who had helped them (however we may deplore his actions) gives another unflattering sidelight on the kind of people they were (Matthew 27:3 – 10).

So by teasing out this one thread and following it, we can show how John demonstrates the rising tension between 'the Jews' and the Lord Jesus. Each scene shows a steady escalation of the conflict over time, and introduces new facets to both sides of the dispute. However, John rarely comments on how people feel or states directly that 'hostility is growing', he tells us what people do and say and leaves us to draw our own conclusions. This way 'the Jews' move stepwise from asking reasonable questions to plotting murder, and their *coup de grace* is to get someone else to do it for them.

The Gospel of John is often described as being a major source of Christian anti-Semitism, in that he shows 'the Jews' as the main force behind the death of Jesus. Whilst there is not space to go into this in detail, it should be obvious from the above study that whilst *some* Jews clearly were deeply involved in bringing about Jesus' death, this could not have been any and all Jews. For what John is actually showing us is that they are as diverse a group of people as any other.

4.
The Ticking Clock.

4. The Ticking Clock.

In John's Gospel, the whole span of the Ages, and more, are put before us. From John 1:1 NIV 'In the beginning...' to John 21:23 NIV 'until I return', time and again John uses aspects of this theme to grab our attention and make us think. In the last chapter we saw how events of escalating antagonism are arranged in a linear manner, showing how tension increases as time goes on.

Aligned with this is the related but different idea of the importance of time itself in that escalation, the impression that time is running out which pervades the whole Gospel. If you had never read any of the Gospels and knew nothing about the events, you would still be conscious that time is passing, that it's limited, and that it's leading towards a devastating climax. It's easy to miss this use of time if we are very familiar with John's Gospel, because this type of evocation works only once.

To draw a literary analogy, John has created within his text a sense of suspense. The technique is referred to as a 'ticking clock', a clearly anachronistic device in first century Palestine and almost as out of place in the 21st century! But though silent time-measuring devices are everywhere in our modern world, it's still considered bad practice for a writer to have people constantly checking their wrist or their phone to find out how much time they've got left to save the world. Like John two thousand years ago, he or she must think of other ways to launch the narrative into overdrive.

We have already looked at the various words that are used in the Greek language to express the idea of time, and I would now like to refresh your mind about the word '*horah*' which is significant in this context: *horah* (G5610) means an hour, a day, an instant (literally or figuratively). It may be translated 'hour' but more modern translations often use 'time', or an estimate of the time of day.

The Use of the Word *horah* in Matthew, Mark and Luke.

Although this word is used in the Synoptic Gospels, it is not used as frequently and almost never in the same way that it is used in John's Gospel. The three main uses are:

1) To indicate temporal proximity, i.e. the event is happening now or within a short time interval, e.g. 'that very hour', (Matthew 15:28, Mark 13:11, and Luke 20:19).

2) To give an indication of the time of day, e.g. 'from the sixth hour', (Matthew 27:45, Mark 15:25, Luke 1:10).

3) To give a portentous warning: 'the hour is near'. This occurs only once in Matthew and Mark, and although the Lord seems to be giving a warning, the disciples with Him are asleep (Matthew 26:45; Mark 14:41). Luke does not use the word in this way.

The Use of the Word *horah*, in John's Gospel.

In John's Gospel, *horah* is occasionally used in the more common way, to indicate temporal proximity, (only once, 19:27), or to indicate the time of day, (four times, 1:39; 4:52; 11:9; 19:14). The most frequent usage, however, comes in the 'ominous warning' category, which will be explored in detail below.

The Fateful Hour

This is always in view in this Gospel, and refers not just to a short period of time but metaphorically to the climactic events of Jesus' glorification. It is first mentioned on the occasion of the Lord's first public miracle:

> John 2:4 KJV Jesus saith unto her, Woman, what have I to do with thee? mine hour is not yet come.

Jesus seems to have consciously regulated His ministry in view of that 'hour', and neither friend nor foe could do anything about it.

Linked in with this is the idea that there is a 'right time' for things to happen and that we have to accept this and wait for it. Also we must try to differentiate between what seems like a good time for us, and what God has planned. The fact that even Jesus had to accept this, explains why throughout much of His ministry, He seems to avoid attracting attention. He works miracles, and then commands people not to talk about it. He sees trouble coming and moves on. Many people find this rather odd, as did the Lord's brothers at the beginning of John 7. But Jesus tells them, 'The right time for me has not yet come; for you any time is right.'

So we have the idea of the World's time, and God's time. God, we believe, was aiming for a particular Passover, so He did not want Jesus to attract opposition from the Jews too soon.[15]

The references to the 'Fateful Hour' of John's Gospel can be

---

[15] See 'Life Through His Name' p 249.

divided into two groups:

1. The Hour of Change. The hour that is coming, when things are going to change, e.g.:

> John 4:21 KJV Jesus saith unto her, Woman, believe me, the hour cometh, when ye shall neither in this mountain, nor yet at Jerusalem, worship the Father. (See also 4:23; 5:25, 28; 9:4; 16:2, 4, 25, 32).

2. The Hour of the Lord. The hour to which all of His earthly life has been building up, and which for most of the gospel has 'not yet come'. It is possible to arrange those references which seem to be directly concerned with 'the Lord's hour' into a simple pattern of seven units with a turning point in the centre.[16]

Table 1: The Lord's Hour.

---

[16] This kind of pattern is often found in Scripture, (see 'Motive, Method and Opportunity'). In this case we can also see a connecting theme of 'glory' associated with the beginning, central and end sections which shows another feature of such a pattern, see Chapter 5 below.

	Location	References (KJV)
The Hour is Not Yet Come.	Cana in Galilee. A wedding feast.	John 2:4 Jesus saith unto her, Woman, what have I to do with thee? mine **hour** is not yet come.
	Jerusalem, Temple area.	John 7:30 ... no man laid hands on him, because his **hour** was not yet come.
	Jerusalem, Temple area.	John 8:20 ... and no man laid hands on him; for his **hour** was not yet come.
The Turning Point.	Prior to Passover, Jerusalem. Some Greeks ask to speak to Jesus. Philip and Andrew consult Him about this.	John 12:23 And Jesus answered them, saying, The **hour** is come, that the Son of man should be glorified...
		John 12:27a Now is my soul troubled; and what shall I say? Father, save me from this **hour**:
		John 12:27b but for this cause came I unto this **hour**.
The Hour is Come, when...	Prior to Passover, Jerusalem.	John 13:1 ... when Jesus knew that his **hour** was come that he should depart out of this world unto the Father...
	Prior to Passover, Jerusalem.	John 16:32 Behold, the **hour** cometh, yea, is now come, that ye shall be scattered...
	Prior to Passover, Jerusalem.	John 17:1a These words spake Jesus, and lifted up his eyes to heaven, and said, Father, the **hour** is come;

In Table 1 I have quoted the KJV because the NIV translates 'hour' as 'time' in some cases thus losing the comparative sense.

The turning point occurs *after* the raising of Lazarus, *after* the dinner where Mary anoints Jesus' feet, *after* the Lord rides into Jerusalem on an ass's colt to great acclaim from the crowds, *after* the Pharisees start to get really twitchy, then finally we arrive at the climax of all these events: the feast of the Passover which God had in mind all along.

It's not difficult to understand why the feast of the Passover was chosen by God as a suitable time for Christ's sacrifice to occur. What is not so clear is why *that particular* Passover? Space does not permit a full answer to this question, and in any case it is still a subject of debate, so I will simply list three areas of interest:

1) Astronomical and calendar considerations show that, if the crucifixion took place on Friday 14th Nissan in the Jewish calendar, it could have occurred on Friday 7th April 30 CE, or on Friday 3rd April 33 CE. The latter date also coincides with a lunar eclipse. This eclipse would have been visible from Jerusalem and would have caused the moon to appear blood red, which some scholars have linked with Peter's reference to the prophet Joel in Acts 2:20.[17]

2) Prophetic factors centre on the Book of Daniel, (Daniel 9:21 – 27). There are many interpretations of the numbers given in this prophecy, but most scholars agree that the 'Anointed One' refers to Jesus Christ and that 'cut off' refers to His crucifixion (9:26).[18]

---

[17] See Humphreys, 'The Mystery of the Lord's Supper'.
[18] For an idea of the complexities involved here see Penny's book, 'Daniel's Seventy Sevens'.

3) According to John's account, the Jewish authorities did not have the right to execute people at the time they arrested Jesus (18:31). This right may have been removed by the Roman authorities around 30 CE, but there is no clear documentary evidence. It is therefore possible that this was the first Passover where the Roman method of execution, crucifixion, was an option.[19]

Many Jews, both local and from further afield, would be in Jerusalem for the Feast. Included in the throng are a group of 'Greeks'(12:20). The oddity of the arrival of the Greeks is something to note if not explain. They ask Philip if they can 'see' Jesus. Philip and Andrew tell Jesus about them, but His 'reply' does not seem to answer their question. Whether the Greeks ever got to see Him, up close and personal, we are not told. Neither are we told the implication of their arrival, but are left with a niggling feeling that there is one and that, because of Jesus' reply, it is significant.[20] But what exactly is the meaning of the arrival of this fateful hour, the Lord's Hour, that has finally come?

---

[19] The Jerusalem Talmud records that the right of execution was removed roughly '40 years before the destruction of the Temple'. The Jews obviously had some jurisdiction over crimes that involved their religion, and they were clearly prepared to imply the death penalty with threats (John 8:5, 8:59, 10:31) but such stonings may not have been legal.

[20]See: 'The Coming of the Greeks' in Welch's 'Life Through His Name' p 342.

5.

The Lord's Hour

5. The Lord's Hour

The period of time referred to as the Lord's Hour is one of considerable importance, but examining every aspect would occupy many pages. Most Scripture can be read on several levels and with varying attention to detail, and this is an excellent example of that. Therefore, what follows is more like the tip of an iceberg than a complete investigation. To begin, then, what can we learn about the Lord's Hour based on the work we've already done?

1) 'The Lord's Hour' has been anticipated throughout the Gospel up until John 12:23. It is a figure of speech rather than a period of 60 minutes (compare 16:21). The word 'hour' is, in this case, always represented by the Greek word *horah*, which was defined on p. 30 and can be used in a precise or loose way.

2) This 'Hour' is the climax of Jesus' whole ministry, of His entire human life. It's the reason He's here.

3) Jesus has it in mind right from the start. We can see this as early as John 2:4 where He tells His mother that 'my hour is not yet come'.

4) There is no doubt Jesus knew *what* this Hour would bring (John 2:19 – 22; 3:14; 12:7, 24, 27, 32, 33; 13:1; 18:4), though John is rather more subtle than the Synoptic writers (Matthew 20:17 – 19; Mark 8:31; Luke 9:22).

5) Right after the Greeks ask to see Him, Jesus describes 'the Hour' Himself in this telling sound-bite: 'The hour has come for the Son of Man to be glorified'.

6) The timing is part of God's design, and Jesus must not deviate from this. In John 7: 1 – 9 His brothers may be mocking Him somewhat, but I think genuine puzzlement has prompted their reaction. They do not understand that their view of a marvellous photo-opportunity may not coincide with God's plan. So we see Jesus slowing things down to avoid being arrested too soon (John 8:59; 10:39), and at the appropriate moment, speeding Judas on his way (13:27). Timing is crucial and Jesus plays an essential part in making sure that it's just right.

This means we can say with certainty that the basic events of what happens in and as a result of 'the Lord's Hour' are not a surprise to Jesus. He knows that He will be betrayed, arrested, wrongfully convicted, subjected to verbal and physical abuse, and finally, having taken on the sin of the whole world, He will endure one of the most humiliating and painful deaths that man has ever devised.

The Events of the Lord's Hour.

John reports Jesus' words (12:23) to inform us that 'the hour has come'. That this hour is not a point in time but a span of time is indicated by the repetition of this statement (John 13:1 and 17:1). But just as John does not enumerate all the signs, neither does he tell us exactly what events the Lord's Hour might be considered to include. The following, which assumes that John's text is chronological, is a brief overview of the possibilities:

1) Jesus speaking to the assembled crowd; the voice from heaven (John 12:23 – 50).

2) The evening meal before the Passover Feast; the foot-washing; the betrayal by Judas (John 13).

3) The Upper Room Discourse; Jesus preparing His disciples for the forthcoming ordeal (John 14 – 16).

4) Jesus' praying to the Father that He will protect the disciples (John 17).

5) Jesus and His disciples crossing the Kidron Valley and entering the olive grove (John 18:1).

6) Judas and his band of men arriving, followed by Jesus' arrest (John 18:2 – 13).

7) Jesus before the Authorities, both Jewish and Gentile (John 18:14 – 19:16).

8) The Crucifixion (John 19:16 – 37).

I have not included the resurrection because I feel there is a critical aspect to 'the Lord's Hour'. There is a point beyond which there is no going back, and that must surely be Jesus' death on the cross, the 'crisis' (usually translated 'judgement') of John 12:31.

A crossing and a crisis: John 18:1.

If you keep a diary, you'll have noticed that mostly you do not write in 'real time' but vary the wording according to the importance of the details. One word, 'Boring!' may sum up a routine and humdrum day, but if the next day you meet the love of your life, the description of the same timespan might run to pages. Of course, this applies to other kinds of writing as well, and there are also other reasons for varying the word-count. Writers must consider physical things like how much space is available and how portable the work needs to be. Sometimes a topic might be restricted for fear of the manuscript falling into the wrong hands.

Another limitation impinges on literary style. To stop the text meandering, a writer may choose a particular idea as an anchor. This means he or she may exclude details that either seem irrelevant to or do not support this theme, irrespective of whether they consider them to be important or interesting in their own right.

With this in mind, plus the fact that much has been written by others on most of the subjects listed above, I decided to focus on a span of time which most commentaries either miss out entirely or briefly skip over. This is the period which is compressed into just one verse at the beginning of Chapter 18.

> John 18:1 NIV When he had finished praying, Jesus left with his disciples and crossed the Kidron Valley. On the other side there was an olive grove, and he and his disciples went into it.

I chose it because at first it reads like one of those unremarkable paragraphs whose function is to ensure that the last scene flows smoothly into the next. Looking more closely, however, especially if you have also read the Synoptic versions of this period, you begin to notice curiosities.

In fact, this verse is a brilliant example of how a couple of seemingly inconsequential sentences can be shown to have echoes that resonate with both contextual and historic events, not to mention the writer's agenda. Finding these things out not only helps our understanding of what's going on at that time, but broadens our Biblical knowledge as well.

The time covered by 18:1 is sandwiched between the Great Prayer of Chapter 17, and the arrival at the olive grove of Judas. We are told of his knowledge of the place, and that he arrives leading a group of soldiers and officials (18:2 – 3). The narrative drive sweeps us away from that brief introduction which seems insignificant compared with what is to follow.

The fact is, if we had no other gospel but John's, we would assume that nothing of interest happens in the olive grove, for as soon as the interlopers arrive, Jesus goes out of it to talk to them (John 18:4). This is strange, because the Synoptic gospels' account of what happens there occupies a significant amount of time and would seem to be of considerable importance. Indeed it is so fraught and disturbing it is often referred to as the 'Agony in the Garden'.

The absence of this scene[21] will puzzle any reader or hearer who is familiar with the other stories about Jesus' final hours, especially since the author of John's Gospel is supposed to have been there. It puzzled me; and my growing conviction that there is more to 18:1 than meets the eye caused me to wonder if what John does not say might sometimes be as important as what he

---

[21] The Temptation in the Wilderness and the Transfiguration are also significant omissions, and there are other discrepancies in the events recorded by John: see Anderson's The Riddles of the Fourth Gospel, Chapter 3 and also Lincoln's commentary, pages 26 – 38 on 'Relation to the Synoptic Gospels' which describes the history of thought as to how the Gospel of John was written, and covers the point about whether or not John had access to and used the Synoptics.

does say. Readers of Arthur Conan Doyle may remember the famous clue of the dog in the night-time.

'But the dog did nothing in the night-time!' protests the Scotland Yard Detective.

'Exactly,' says Sherlock Holmes. 'The dog should have barked the place down. Why didn't he?'

So What Does John 18:1 Actually Say?

Variant translations into English exist throughout Scripture. They are caused either by variations in the original manuscripts being translated, or by the differing opinions of the groups of translators involved.

Although John 18:1 would seem to be a straightforward piece of prose, different translations exist. As far as I can discover, these changes do not reflect differences in the Greek originals, but their presence has subtly altered the significance of the passage. In Table 2 I have broken the verse down into three sections and compared the NIV with the LITV,[22] as these two translations highlight the differences very well. Following the table, I consider each one by comparing it with the equivalent Synoptic section.

---

[22] In the LITV, Jay P Green used the Greek Textus Receptus. The NIV translators used a combination of the latest Greek language editions of the United Bible Societies. I have also looked at the Nestle-Aland Greek text. In this case all the Greek texts seem to be similar.

Table 2: Variant Translations of John 18:1

John 18:1		
	NIV	**LITV**
1.	When he had finished praying	Having said these things
2.	Jesus left with his disciples and crossed the Kidron Valley	Jesus went out with His disciples across the winter stream Kidron
3.	On the other side there was an olive grove and he and his disciples went into it	where there was a garden into which He and His disciples entered

Section 1: This section is not immediately relevant to this study, so I shall pass straight on to section 2.

Section 2: Jesus went out with His disciples across the winter stream Kidron.

The Synoptic Gospels mention the Mount of Olives and Gethsemane, names that go together since 'Gethsemane' means 'oil press'. But John ignores both. Instead he speaks of the Kidron Valley, and by so doing takes us time-travelling backwards for roughly a thousand years. So first let's look at the geography of the area for a moment. If you have a map of Jerusalem and its surroundings, that will help.[23]

Jerusalem is situated on a ridge that forms the backbone of Judea. It has a strong defensive position, with the Kidron Valley to the east and the Hinnom Valley to the south and west. To the east of

---

[23] See The Times Concise Atlas of the Bible, p 117 or The Holman Bible Atlas, p 229.

the city is the Mount of Olives, upon whose lower western slopes we assume stood the place called Gethsemane, which John refers to as a garden. Its precise location is unclear, though tradition places it opposite the Temple.

Crossing the Kidron Valley is therefore essential to get to the garden or grove, but it would not have been an unusual journey for Jesus to make. He would have crossed it to get to Bethany, and then in the opposite direction when He came riding back into Jerusalem 'on a colt, the foal of a donkey'. The question is, why does John mention it when the Synoptic Gospels do not?

The clue is in the precise wording. Most translations have the word 'brook', 'stream' or 'valley', but John's description of the Kidron is 'winter-flowing'. This same phrase is used in the LXX 2 Samuel 15:23, where King David, betrayed by his son Absalom and his counsellor Ahithophel, flees across the 'winter-flowing Kidron' from Jerusalem to the Mount of Olives. There, in great distress, he prays to the Lord for help.[24] A further link is provided by the fact that Jesus had, just a few days earlier, been acclaimed as the King of Israel (John 12:12 – 13). Also, crossing the Kidron is associated with bringing death upon oneself. Though this situation in no other way parallels Jesus' predicament, the wording is interesting:

> 1Kings 2:37 NIV The day you leave and cross the Kidron Valley, you can be sure you will die; your blood will be on your own head.

The Kidron Valley is mentioned several more times in the Old Testament, as the main place for disposing of heathen images and idols (1 Kings 15:13; 2 Chronicles 29:16; 2 Kings 23:4,6,12).

---

[24] See Lincoln pp 442, 443.

King Josiah also had human bones placed on the slope of the Mount of Olives (2 Kings 23:14), and the valley became a place of tombs. Jeremiah 31:40 speaks of it as the valley where dead bodies and ashes were thrown.[25]

The valley is also well placed for receiving effluent from the city. A main drainage tunnel from the Second Temple period was discovered in 2007. The Temple itself used a huge amount of water for purification purposes, and slaughtered many animals, particularly during Passover. A sewer at the south-west corner of the altar carried the blood and rinsing water to the Kidron valley.[26]

As the stream flowed only during winter rains, it seems likely that at the time of the Passover there would be little natural water there. Due to all the debris dumped there over the years, it would also have been much deeper then than it is today. It's possible there was a bridge,[27] but even so, when it was crossed by Jesus and the disciples, especially if they had to cross downstream of the Temple drains, it could easily have been an experience redolent of blood and death.

Another aspect to consider is the meaning of the name Kidron. In Hebrew, it comes from the verb *qadar* which means to be ashy or dark coloured, or to mourn. Altogether, there's a lot of

---

[25] The Kidron is also linked with the Valley of Jehoshaphat as the place of final judgement (Joel 3:2), but the link is tenuous.
[26] The Cambridge History of Judaism: The Early Roman Period, page 55.
[27] Some of the temple rituals involved crossing to the Mount of Olives. There is textual evidence for an elaborate bridge, see Mishnah Parah 3:6 which begins, 'they made a causeway from the Temple Mount to the Mount of Olives'. However no archaeological evidence has been found for this.

significance in the name for anyone well-acquainted with the Hebrew Bible.

Section 3: There was a garden, and Jesus and His disciples entered it.
This is all John says about the experience in the garden at this point. I therefore decided I must take a diversion into the Synoptics and find out what it is that John is so conspicuously not saying.

The Synoptic Version

The three accounts are similar but differ in detail. I see this as an example of different observers or documenters recording different aspects of what happened. To get the full impact you should read it yourself (Matthew 26:36 – 46; Mark 14:32 – 42; Luke 22:39 – 47) and construct your own integration of the three accounts. Here is a very simplified summary:

Though the garden is familiar to Jesus, when He enters it He begins to feel uneasy. He splits the disciples up, taking Peter, James and John with Him. He tells them to wait, to watch, and to pray, and then moves away from them too. Now alone, He prays to the Father. He prays three times overall. The object of the prayers is similar but the intensity escalates. The Father's intervention is requested. A disaster, described as 'the cup'[28], is about to overtake the Lord Jesus and only the Father can prevent it. But this interference must be at the Father's discretion, and

---

[28] In addition to its obvious meaning as a drinking vessel, the 'cup' is also used in Scripture as a figure of speech pertaining to a person's fate (Psalm 16:5). It can be used positively, (Psalm 16:5; 23:5; 116:13), but more often it is used negatively (Isaiah 51:17; Jeremiah 25:15; Revelation 14:10).

Jesus' distress is acute. He falls with His face to the ground, is strengthened by an angel, and sweats drops of blood. His closest disciples fail Him; they fail to do as He asks, to wait, watch and pray, and they fall asleep.

Another way to crystallise what's happening is to consider not only the events but Jesus' emotions and the effect they have on Him. Looking at the actual words used by the Synoptic Gospel writers we can form the following picture:

1) On moving into the garden Jesus *begins* to be sorrowful (*lupeo*, G3076: Matthew 26:37).

2) This rapidly progresses to being in distress of mind (*ademoneo* G85: Matthew 26:37; Mark 14:33), the only use of this word in the gospels. It seems to mean much more than just being very sad. Full to the brim with sadness might be a reasonable description.

3) Mark alone uses the word *ekthambeo* (G1568; Mark 14:33), which means that Jesus was 'utterly astonished', possibly even 'greatly affrighted'. Mark uses it of people who are alarmed or amazed on encountering something unexpected (Mark 9:15; 16:5).

4) Jesus then becomes 'exceeding sorrowful even unto death' *(perilupos* G4036; Matthew 26:38; Mark 14:34). This seems to go a step further. The grief is not only filling Him up but it's all around Him as well. It's so powerful He thinks it might kill Him.

5) We can then add Luke's observation (Luke 22:44) that Jesus is experiencing anguish so great He's sweating

blood.[29] The word translated 'anguish' is *agonia* (G74). It more usually implies struggle or conflict, and Paul uses it this way (e.g. 2 Timothy 4:7). So it could be that Jesus is involved in a conflict so harrowing, and is praying so intently, that He experiences an acute stress response. This causes the rupture of capillary blood vessels, leaking blood into the sweat glands. The phenomenon is rare but is known to occur in conditions of extreme emotional or physical stress.

There are various theories as to what was going on, and interested readers should study the references and Internet links on the subject.[30] Many have also wondered who the observers were if the disciples were asleep, but this is not a path I intend to explore in this study. Clearly either someone else was watching or Jesus told His disciples later.

So what can we make of this? Here is our Lord Jesus Christ, approaching the climax of His entire ministry, and He's what? Sad? Anxious? Distressed? Astonished? Afraid? Overwhelmed? Conflicted? Distraught? Dying? All of the above?

Our first response, on reading this litany of distress, is to wonder: 'What kind of incident could possibly have made our Lord so troubled?'

And our second question, in the context of this study, is surely to

---

[29] Luke 22:43 – 44 does not appear in the earliest manuscripts, but in later quotations. Its authenticity is therefore debated by some scholars.

[30] A description of what may have happened in Gethsemane is given by Welch and Allen in 'Perfection and Perdition' Chapter 5, pp 210 – 217, by Felter in 'Gethsemane' and much more concisely by Sylvia Penny in 'Satan in Gethsemane'.

ask: 'Why does John appear to ignore this apparently devastating event?'

These two questions are connected, and I would like to look at the second one first.

Why Does John Miss it Out?

Before we begin I would like to emphasize that throughout the following discussion the only thing we can be sure about is that John does not include the 'Agony in the Garden' scene as part of his account. All the rest is conjecture from available evidence. With this in mind, let us consider the main reason commentators give for the omission: that John is working to a different agenda from the Synoptic Gospels, and an important difference is that his central theme, his 'anchor', is to emphasize the glory and exaltation of Christ.

The Companion Bible states that although Jesus is presented in the Synoptic Gospels to show His perfect humanity, John's purpose, inspired by the Holy Spirit, is to say 'Behold your God.' Hence, there is no Agony in the Garden, for it would have been out of place in a gospel concerned with presenting Jesus' heavenly and eternal glory.[31] The Oxford Bible Commentary agrees, stating that John left out this scene because he intended to portray the Lord's Hour not as a time of humiliation but as one of glorification and exaltation. We can see this exemplified in Table 3 below.

Throughout the Gospel, John's perspective also emphasises that things do not happen to Jesus by coincidence or by accident.

---

[31] 'The Companion Bible', the introduction to John's Gospel; p 1510.

Rather the Trinity, through Jesus' actions, is orchestrating events. He takes the initiative and the people He encounters react to Him:

1) He aims to determine the hour of His death. This is implied by all the references to the fact that His 'hour is not yet come', and underscored by John 10:17 – 18.

2) He selects people, including some of those He is going to heal (John 5:6; 9:1; 6:70; 13:18; 15:16,19).

3) He willingly crosses the Kidron valley, though the garden is a place He is known to frequent. When the arresting officers arrive, He goes out to meet them and asks what they want (John 18:4).

Therefore, if John's intention is to portray the Lord's Hour exclusively as one of glorification, exaltation and forward planning, his exclusion of the 'Agony in the Garden' implies that this event is one that the Lord did not plan. That here the initiative is taken from Him, and that for a while, this person or event has Jesus on the wrong foot. I feel this is an important clue as to what really happened in the garden. It is why, if you like, the dog did not bark.

Table 3: The Lord's Hour and its relationship to His glory.

	References (KJV)	The Glory Link (NIV)
The Hour Is Not Yet Come.	Wedding at Cana in Galilee, the first sign.	
	'Mine **hour** is not yet come' (2:4)	The result of this sign is that 'He thus revealed his **glory**;' (2:11)
The Turning Point.	Prior to Feast of Passover, after the arrival of the Greeks.	
	'The **hour** is come' (12: 23). 'Father, save me from this **hour**: but for this cause came I unto this **hour**.' (12:27)	'for the Son of man to be **glorified**.' (12: 23) 'Father, **glorify** your name.' Then a voice came from heaven, 'I have **glorified** it, and will **glorify** it again.' (12:28)
The Hour is Come	Just before Passover, after the evening meal.	
	These words spake Jesus, and lifted up his eyes to heaven, and said, 'Father, the **hour** is come;' (17:1)	'**glorify** your Son, that your Son may **glorify** you.' (17:1)

However, while the dog does not bark, it occasionally growls a little. John also side-steps two other main scenes, the Temptations and the Transfiguration, but while they *appear* to be absent, this may not be completely true. Many believe that John 1:14 and 12:27 – 33 allude to the Transfiguration; that John chose to depict that event as a couple of suggestions rather than one overwhelming scene. We can also see echoes of the Temptations in the Feeding of the 5000 (6:1 – 15) where the provision of miraculous food *could* have been used by Jesus to create a huge following for all the wrong reasons, to achieve the wrong kind of kingdom in the wrong way.

So it's possible that although John has omitted the 'Agony in the Garden' because it does not chime with his objectives, still he realises that the other gospel accounts are incomplete and has left us hints throughout the text as to what is going on:

1) We have the naming of the Kidron Valley and its Old Testament associations. This provides a link to the Synoptic accounts, which also tie in Judas' treachery to Ahitophel's betrayal of David via Psalm 41:9 (Matthew 26:23; Mark 14:20; Luke 22:21; John 13:18).

2) There are several clues that point to the fact that Jesus was totally committed to doing the Father's will (John 4:34; 5:30; 6:38; 8:29). This supports the tone of Jesus' prayers in the garden that 'not my will but Yours be done', which occurs in all three Synoptic accounts.

3) Thirdly, we have the clue that comes in John 12, after the arrival of the Greeks and Jesus' announcement that 'The hour has come':

John 12:27 NIV 'Now my heart is troubled, and what shall I say? "Father, save me from this hour?" No, it was for this very reason I came to this hour.'

Here John assures us of Jesus' determination to see it through. 'Would I ever ask such a thing?' Jesus seems to be saying. 'This hour is the reason I'm here!' So, *we* might reasonably ask, why then does He admit that his 'heart is troubled'?

The Greek word *tarasso*, translated 'troubled' (G5015, meaning to stir, agitate or roil) is used in the Gospel seven times. The first two references concern the Pool of Bethesda whose waters were 'troubled' or stirred up from time to time (5:4,7; thought by some to be a later addition). The last two occur in Chapter 14 where Jesus exhorts His disciples: 'let not your hearts be troubled' (14:1,27). The three central occurrences, however, pertain to Jesus Himself, as detailed in Table 4 below.

Table 4: Occasions when Jesus is Troubled.

Occasion and Reference	What exactly is troubled?
1. The Death of Lazarus: 11:33 (NIV).	His spirit (*pneuma* G4151) is deeply moved and troubled.
2. After arrival of the Greeks: John 12:27 (NIV).	His heart (*psuche* G5590) is troubled. This is the only time in this gospel that Jesus *says* He is troubled.
3. Imminent betrayal by Judas Iscariot, John 13:21 (NIV).	His spirit (*pneuma* G4151) is troubled.

So verse 12:27 is unusual. It's the only verse in John's Gospel where the Lord Jesus plainly mentions being troubled. But what exactly is it about Him that is troubled? His heart (NIV)? His soul (KJV)? Is there a difference?

Look at verse 12:25. Here the same word in Greek is used (*psuche* G5590), this time translated not as 'heart' but as 'life'. In fact, the word occurs ten times in John's Gospel and eight times it is translated 'life'.

In the Bible many things go in threes and in John's Gospel, 'life' is one of them. Indeed the idea of life is so important we could investigate it as another theme, were there space to do so.[32] Such a study would conclude that John, in his gospel, describes three types of life:

(1) Life which stands alone, '*zoe*' (G2222) e.g. John 1:4.

(2) Aionion (or eternal or everlasting) Life where the word '*aionios*' (G166) is always coupled with '*zoe*' (G2222) e.g. John 17:3.

(3) Human Life, *psuche,* (G5590) e.g. John 13:37.

Now the translation of this '*psuche*-life' is debatable and as we have seen above, it has been translated 'life', 'heart' or 'soul'. But whichever is used, it seems to describe our life as a living, breathing human being. The good shepherd gives his human life for the sheep (10:11). Peter declares he will give up his human life for Jesus (13:37). So it makes sense to conclude that whatever is troubling Jesus, it's something to do with His human life.

4) John alone refers to Gethsemane as a garden. Like the naming of the Kidron Valley, this also could be an Old Testament allusion. In this case it links to the garden of Eden, where the original Adam[33], having eaten the forbidden fruit, realises his human life is most definitely on the line (Genesis 3).

---

[32] Aspects of this are considered in detail in a forthcoming booklet: 'The Theme of Time in the Gospel of John, Part 2'.
[33] Paul describes Jesus as the last Adam, 1 Corinthians 15:45.

5) John 18:11 is also put forward by some commentaries[34] as a subtle reference to the 'Agony in the Garden'.

> John 18:11 NIV Jesus commanded Peter, 'Put your sword away! Shall I not drink the cup the Father has given me?'

While the idea of 'drinking the cup' does put us in mind of that scene, there is a difference. In the Synoptic account Jesus three times asks the Father to 'take away the cup', the dreadful fate that He fears may await Him, but He never says that particular cup was *given* to Him by the Father. Also, there is the testimony in Hebrews:

> Hebrews 5:7 NIV During the days of Jesus' life on earth, he offered up prayers and petitions with loud cries and tears to the one who could save him from death, and he was heard because of his reverent submission.

This implies that, at some point, Jesus prayed to be saved from death and was 'heard'. Other Scriptures show that being heard is synonymous with having one's petition granted (2 Kings 20:5; 2 Chronicles 7:12; Psalm 6:9; Luke 1:13; Acts 10:31). There is no reference to Jesus having prayed to be saved from anything except in the garden of Gethsemane. So God must have heard His prayer and saved Him from drinking that particular cup.

On the other hand, in John 18:11, Jesus clearly implies that He *is* going to drink the cup. He's going to go through with it! There's no trace of hesitation. Perhaps John is emphasizing that, for the cup *that the Father had given Him*, hesitation had never been an option.

---

[34] e.g. the Oxford Commentary p 993.

Thus we can conclude that although John sidesteps time and leaves out the scene in Gethsemane, its inclusion as a series of allusions gives us a sidelight on what really happened there:

1) The period of time that John misses out is linked to the Synoptic accounts by an Old Testament allusion, Psalm 41.

2) Jesus was totally committed to doing the Father's will.

3) His human life was what was at stake in the garden.

4) This is backed up by an allusion to the Garden of Eden and the first Adam.

5) Jesus never had any hesitation in accepting the 'cup' of death on the cross. What happened in the garden was about death, yes, but not that one.

So what did happen in the Garden?

Though this is the next question that comes to mind, its investigation must be left for another day. My 'anchor' for this study is 'the Theme of Time in the Gospel of John', and John decided he would not spend time describing the events in detail so I must do the same.

John's objective was to show that Jesus is the Christ, to emphasize His glory and exaltation, to show that He is a person who orchestrates things, people, even the weather, and is totally in control of the situation. But the events in the garden do not fit this pattern. Why? Because for a short time, it appears that Jesus is *not* in control. His human life is threatened. If He could have got

Himself out of it He would have. It's an unexpected occurrence that He does not know how to tackle other than by asking the Father to intervene.

It's as if John's saying, 'Okay, it was desperate for a while but they got it sorted, and really that's all we need to know. But for those of you who love a puzzle, here's a few pointers to set you on the right track...'

As a final thought I would like to consider the following:

> John 10:17-18 NIV The reason my Father loves me is that I lay down my life —only to take it up again. No one takes it from me, but I lay it down of my own accord. I have authority to lay it down and authority to take it up again. This command I received from my Father.

How does this square with Jesus' constant planning, His avoidance of the authorities, or with the scene in the garden where we are proposing He might be on the verge of death? If He can voluntarily take His life up again, why is He so worried about losing it in the garden? If He can recover from being crucified, surely He can also be miraculously healed from even the most devastating attack?

I don't know the answer for certain of course, but I would like to suggest that this is because the resurrection process took time. After the crucifixion, Jesus does not immediately return to life 'as if by magic'. When He does, He warns Mary against touching Him (John 20:17), and even a week later His wounds are still clearly visible (John 20:26 – 27). We have seen that this particular Passover was crucial; everything had been set up for it. It was the culmination of years of careful planning; it could not be allowed to go wrong.

As I said in the introduction: time is an Enemy, and never more so than here. But the Enemy was not allowed to prevail. Instead, the Lord's Hour presented the world with the most stunning visual public event of the whole Gospel story, the crucifixion. Its horror and its glory have echoed round the world for two thousand years.

6.
Conclusions.

6. Conclusions.

The Theme of Time in John's Gospel has brought into focus the following ideas:

1. Time is an important aspect of John's text. Whether or not he deliberately set out to make it so is a question we cannot answer, but if we believe that he wrote by inspiration of the Holy Spirit, its significance cannot be in doubt.

2. John uses time at every level from telling us the time of day (it was the sixth hour) to the time of year (it was winter). Sometimes he slows narrative time by giving us much information (John 13 – 17), only to then collapse it and miss out an event completely (John 18:1). Time is used for emotional effects (why didn't you get here sooner?) and forms the basis of important theological concepts (eternal life).

3. The importance of 'active waiting' is emphasized by studying several of the signs. Alongside this is the dilemma of when to stop waiting and start acting, and the idea of 'redeeming time' that might otherwise be irretrievably lost. Also it is encouraging to find that even significant disciples like Peter get it wrong, but that this is not necessarily the end of the matter. It is possible to pull yourself together and move on, and your experience of failing may well make you better prepared to encourage others, because you now see more clearly where the problems lie.

4. The progressively escalating nature of the conflict scenes between Jesus and the group of people referred to as 'the Jews' challenges the commonly held belief that John's Gospel was not written chronologically. Indirectly, it also shows us that 'the Jews'

were a diverse group and not all of them were involved in Jesus' death.

5. John uses time as a tool to create suspense: the Ticking Clock. He couples this with the threat of a portentous warning 'the hour is coming'! Reading the Gospel with this in mind:

> (1) Stimulates our emotional perception of what was happening at that time, and helps us to imagine what it was actually like to be there.

> (2) Highlights the importance of timing, of waiting for the 'right time', that this was something even Jesus had to watch out for.

6. Finally the 'right time' arrives and the Lord's Hour has come. John keeps us on track. He does not allow his readers the raft of speculation which often accompanies the 'Agony in the Garden' scene as described by the Synoptics. The important message is that Jesus survives to drink the right cup, at the right time, in the right place. Nevertheless, John is also mindful of the importance of this absent scene and has left clues for the diligent reader.

I hope you have been inspired by this account of how the use of themes can provide new perspectives on our understanding of Scripture, and feel sufficiently curious to proceed to Part 2 which covers 'Stationary Time'. This includes a discussion of the time the Gospel was written, when it was meant to be read, dispensational time, ritual time, time-puzzles, and everlasting life. Also that you will decide to have a go yourself, either to think up your own theme or to apply the Theme of Time to another part of Scripture. In the meantime, I will leave you with a thought concerning the 'Dynamic-Time'-related message of John's Gospel:

The clock is ticking for all of us. In our earthly life, we have access to an abundance of love and grace from the Lord, but we only have so much time. In the past, the focus of that time was the Word being made flesh in the form of Jesus, the events of His ministry, His death, His resurrection, defining moments all. But now that focus is on *us* and depends on *our* defining moment: the moment that we believe. We hold that moment in our hands, we should not put it off for none of us knows what tomorrow may bring. The ticking clock is part of the human condition which Jesus encountered during His life on earth and caused Him to 'work while it is day, for the night is coming'. Do not underestimate the importance of time, for it was an enemy even for the Lord.

Also on John's Gospel

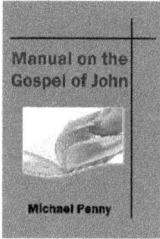

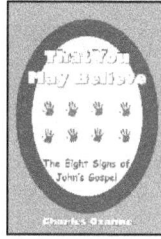
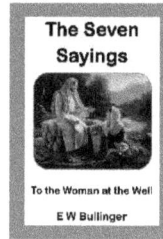

The Manual on the Gospel of John
By Michael Penny

John and the Samaritans
By Brian Sherring

That you may believe
The eight signs in John's Gospel
By Charles Ozanne

The Seven Sayings
To the Woman at the well
E W Bullinger

For further details of the above books, plus others on
John's Gospels, please visit:

www.obt.org.uk

These are available as paperbacks from
The Open Bible Trust
Fordland Mount, Upper Basildon,
Reading, RG8 8LU, UK.

They are also available and as eBooks from Kindle and Apple.
and as KDP paperbacks from Amazon.

About the Author

Eliza Wright was born in Sheffield in 1948 and was educated at Ecclesfield Grammar School. After leaving school she eventually began working at the mental hospital for the area, and qualified as a psychiatric nurse in 1976. A few years later her own health declined, dictating a less physically demanding life-style, and she chose further education.

After obtaining a BSc and PhD in chemistry from Sheffield University, she became a teacher and discovered that teaching was a far more arduous job than nursing. But to compensate for this she met her future husband there. In 1986 she and her husband left teaching and started their own business.

In 1994 they moved to the Isle of Skye where they still reside and are still self-employed in various computer-related areas. Despite her science background, she discovered an unexpected talent for embroidery design. Creating and publishing needlework projects based on the culture and scenery of the Scottish Islands is now her main occupation.

****

Also by Eliza Wright

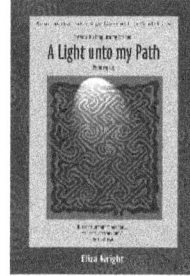

A Light unto my Path

Motive, Method, Opportunity

Details can be seen on

www.obt.org.uk

Available as eBooks from Amazon and Apple and as KDP
paperbacks from Amazon.

Further Reading

Free sample

For a free sample of
the Open Bible Trust's magazine *Search*,
please email admin@obt.org.uk or visit

www.obt.org.uk/search

Bibliography of References:

Anderson, Paul N. 'The Riddles of the Fourth Gospel – An Introduction to John.' Fortress Press, 2011.

Barton, John and Muddiman, John, eds. 'The Oxford Bible Commentary.' Oxford University Press, 2001.

Bauckham, Richard. 'Jesus and the Eyewitnesses.' William B Eerdmans Publishing Co., 2006.

Bauckham, Richard and Mosser, Carl eds. 'The Gospel of John and Christian Theology – Papers from the St Andrews Conference on Scripture and Theology.' William B Eerdmans Publishing Co., 2008.

Companion Bible, The. Kregel Publications.

Cupcea, G. 'Timekeeping in the Roman Army' The Classical Quarterly 67, Issue 2. Cambridge University Press, 2017.

Felter, Peter. 'Gethsemane "My Father, if it is possible, may this cup be taken from Me." Xulon Press, 2012.

Henry, W. M. and Penny, M. 'The Four Gospels Compared and Contrasted.' The Open Bible Trust, 2013.

Hoffmeier, James K. 'The Archaeology of the Bible.' Lion Hudson plc., 2008.

Horbury, William and Davies, W. D. 'The Cambridge History of Judaism: The Early Roman Period.' Cambridge University Press, 1984.

Humphreys C. J. 'The Mystery of the Lord's Supper.' Cambridge University Press, 2011.

Lincoln, Andrew T. 'The Gospel According to Saint John.' Black's New Testament Commentary, Baker Academic, 2005.

Manley, Denis. 'The Chronology of the Gospel of Jesus Christ.' The Open Bible Trust, 2013.

Northumbria Community Trust. 'Celtic Daily Prayer, Book One.'

Penny, Michael: 'Daniel's Seventy Sevens: A Recalculation.' The Open Bible Trust, 2016.

Penny, Sylvia: 'Satan in Gethsemane.' Search No. 187. The Open Bible Trust, 2015.

Richards, E. G. 'Mapping Time – the Calendar and its History.' Oxford University Press, 1998.

Spurgeon C.H. 'Spurgeon's Expository Encyclopaedia.' Marshall Brothers, 1926.

Strong, J. 'Strong's Concordance of the Bible.' (revised by Kohlenberger, J.R. and Swanson, J.A.) Zondervan, 2002.

Vine, W. E. 'Complete Expository Dictionary of Old and New Testament Words.' Thomas Nelson, 1996.

Welch C. H. 'Life Through His Name.' The Berean Publishing Trust, 1953, 1996.

Wright, Eliza. 'Motive, Method and Opportunity: The Fundamental Elements of Bible Study.' The Open Bible Trust, 2018.

About this Book

The Hour is Coming!

The Theme of Time in the Gospel of John

(Part 1)

This study shows the value of 'themes' in the study of Scripture.
That is, take a subject and follow it through. Here the theme of
'time' is looked at throughout John's Gospel.

However, this is more than just a study of 'time'. As she progresses through John's Gospel the author explains what she is doing and why she   is doing it. These methods can then be used and
applied by readers to any specific subjects or particular themes
they may be interested in pursuing.

Publications of The Open Bible Trust must be in accordance with its evangelical, fundamental and dispensational basis. However, beyond this minimum, writers are free to express whatever beliefs they may have as their own understanding, provided that the aim in so doing is to further the object of The Open Bible Trust. A copy of the doctrinal basis is available on **www.obt.org.uk** or from:

THE OPEN BIBLE TRUST
Fordland Mount, Upper Basildon,
Reading, RG8 8LU, UK

www.ingramcontent.com/pod-product-compliance
Lightning Source LLC
Chambersburg PA
CBHW070539030426
42337CB00016B/2264